Recieved
Jan 21, 1997
From May Elbrow.
Kent England

# BEXLEY, BEXLEYHEATH AND WELLING

## A Pictorial History

Dutch Elm Disease strikes Danson Park.

# Bexley, Bexleyheath and Welling

## A Pictorial History

### John Mercer

**Phillimore**

1995

Published by
PHILLIMORE & CO. LTD.
Shopwyke Manor Barn, Chichester, West Sussex

ISBN 1 86077 003 7

Printed and bound in Great Britain by
BIDDLES LTD.
Guildford, Surrey

*To my parents*
*who lived in Bexleyheath*

# List of Illustrations

*Frontispiece:* Danson Park, 1973

# *Acknowledgements*

I wish to thank the following for permission to take, copy or reproduce illustrations in this book: Aerofilms Ltd., 161; A. Bedford, 172; Bexley Civic Society, 12, 15, 17-18, 49-51, 63, 88-9, 122; R. Cornell, 68; J. Davis, 104; L. Dunmow, 127, 131-4, 149, 158-60; M. Fielden, 75, 112, 115, 173, 176-8; R. Gray, 7-8, 11, 52; Local Studies at Hall Place, 5-6, 9, 13-15, 19-23, 25, 27-8, 31-2, 34-5, 37, 38, 39-48, 53, 58, 59-61, 64-6, 69-74, 76-8, 80, 84-5, 87, 91, 93-9, 101-3, 105-110, 113, 116-121, 123-26, 128-9, 135, 143-5, 147-8, 151, 163-66, 168, 170-1; J. Packer, 2, 4, 10, 16, 56, 67, 79, 86, 92, 114, 130, 137-41, 150, 156, 162, 169, 174-5; the late P. Tester, 30, 136, 142, 152-4; Leicester University Press, 24, 54-5. The remainder are my own.

I wish to thank  the staff of the Local Studies Centre of the London Borough of Bexley for their generous help and Jim Packer and Margaret Cufflin for their knowledge and advice. My source material is listed elsewhere.

# Introduction

## Definition of the Area

The old manor of Bexley was well established by the 13th century. The village itself was a substantial one, probably of several score of dwellings. It was one of the largest manors of the kingdom. The little, scattered hamlets of Blendon, Danson, Hurst, Upton and Welling were part of this manor with the parish church of St Mary's providing the spiritual needs of the people. East Wickham was part of the parish of Plumstead until the last century with its own church of St Michael's built for the manor of East Wickham rather than as a parish church. Today East Wickham has been largely swallowed up by Welling and is therefore part of Bexley. Lamorbey was part of Bexley until the turn of the century. This book, therefore, covers the area of the former Borough of Bexley until it was amalgamated with Crayford and Sidcup in 1965.

## Topography

The northern part across Welling and Bexleyheath is an undulating plateau, averaging 125 to 150 feet in elevation. Disturbed Blackheath and Woolwich beds, mostly sands and coarse gravels, overlain here and there with belts of London clay, cover most of it. The sand and gravel beds, which are well-drained, have provided a considerable expanse of suitable building land lying on either side of the old Dover Road running from east to west across the plateau. It forms a low watershed between streams running north across the marshes into the Thames, and the Shuttle flowing south-east into the Cray before it joins the Darent and enters the Thames. Most of the drainage is in this direction, but in the north-east at East Wickham the edge of the plateau is sharply dissected by a number of small valleys indicating northwards towards Woolwich. This was to limit the spread of recent settlement in the East Wickham area.

To the south of the plateau the land falls quite abruptly to the valley of the Cray and its tributary the Shuttle. A spur covered by London clay intervenes between the two streams. Much of this dissected southern area was considered unsuitable for building land until the inter-war years. Since then Green Belt restrictions have held back any comprehensive residential development. Historically the centre of development lay at Bexley in the south-east. Here the flood plain of the Cray narrows and terrace remnants approach close to the river and provided a dry site for the spread of the settlement above the flood plain. This is where the village of Bexley grew. Further south above Bexley the land rises sharply eastwards from the Cray valley up to Dartford Heath. Until the last century the economic and social life of the district followed the Cray and away from the northern plateau.

**Early Development**

On the flood plain of the river Cray east of Hall Place, commercial gravel digging has revealed scatters of small flint blade which seem to be of Mesolithic (Middle Stone Age) origin. Trimmed flakes used to tip arrows have been located in Joyden's Wood. A Neolithic (New Stone Age) flint sickle blade was found at the foot of Shooters Hill and this implies that the growing of corn was practised thereabouts at least four thousand years ago. A greenstone axehead was found in Erith Road, Bexleyheath. This is a rock quite foreign to this area, which denotes that trade crossed the Heath several thousand years ago. On land belonging to Gibson's farm in East Wickham a polished axehead of a very hard grey rock was picked up, again from a source far from this locality. Artifacts from the Bronze Age have also been found. A beautiful flint dagger was discovered in 1953 at a depth of two feet during house building at Eynesford Crescent on the Bexley/Sidcup borders. A hoard of implements which included axeheads, a chisel, a gouge, part of a sword, two spearheads and a knife was found in a gravel pit on the eastern edge of Bexley in 1930.

The Romans built Watling Street from London to Dover which ran over Shooters Hill and across the Heath to Crayford and beyond. No actual remains of the road have been uncovered but it must have been the route now followed by the A207. Not surprisingly a good many discoveries of Roman remains have been made. Burials of cremated remains in pottery urns have been found along the side of the conjectured highway and major excavation has been carried out on buildings and burials next to the *Guy, Earl of Warwick*, in Welling. In Bourne Road, near to the boundary between Bexley and Crayford, the skeleton of a young woman was found in a lead coffin, which bore the decoration of scallop shells symbolising the voyage of the soul across the ocean to the Isles of the Blessed. A similar discovery was made four feet deep at the junction of Wickham Lane and King's Highway. Gold coins were found in Upton and near the *Golden Lion* in the Broadway.

**The Anglo-Saxons**

The earliest written evidence of settlement appears in a charter of A.D.814, when King Cenwulf of Mercia (also ruler of Kent) granted to Archbishop Wulfred 10 ploughlands 'in the place called Bexley', and marked out the boundaries in a way closely corresponding to the Bexley Borough of 1937-65. In this charter also there is a reference to an earthwork (the Faestendic or strong dyke) which can still be traced in Joyden's Wood today. It is conjectured that it was built against possible attack from the west (i.e. the London side) and it may have been built by Anglo-Saxon invaders, fearing a counter-attack from the Romano-Britons who had retreated from their defeat by Hengist at the Battle of Creganford (Crayford) in or about A.D. 456. The ditch, now almost filled in, had a wall behind it and a roadway along which the defenders could move with relative speed.

Some six hundred years later, it is likely that King Harold marched his army along the Roman road crossing the Heath towards Rochester before striking south to meet William the Conqueror near Hastings on 14 October 1066.

**Domesday Book**

Bexley is next heard of as one of the archbishop's own manors in the Domesday Survey of 1086. There were two ploughs which belonged to the demesne (that is land cultivated for the lord's own use), and 56 villagers had between them 10 ploughs. There was a church, three mills worth 48 shillings, eight acres of meadow, and enough woodland to bring in a rent of 100 pigs. These phrases describe only the lord's property but the general picture is of mixed farming in land still heavily wooded. It was a countryside of hamlets, ditches and fences. Irregular arable fields were intermixed with pasture and meadow, and with large patches of woodland. The Heath was not cultivated but the hamlets of Blendon, Danson, Hurst, Upton and Welling either supported some farming or swine were kept in the woods, while the woods were husbanded for timber or for charcoal burning. East Wickham is not mentioned in the Domesday Survey as it was included in the manor of Plumstead.

**Place Names**

The earliest name given to Bexley occurs in the charter of A.D. 814 where it is called 'Byxlea', which probably means the place or clearing associated with box trees. In the Domesday Survey it is known as Bix. By 1240 it had become Bixle, by 1314 Bexle and Bexley by 1610.

Blendon was called 'Bladindon' after the family of John and Maud Bladignone who were buried in St Michael's, East Wickham, but who lived in Blendon, probably on the site of the later Blendon Hall. There is a 1930s road called Bladindon Drive after them.

Welling was called 'Welllyngs' as long ago as 1362, and it is generally agreed that the first part of the name comes from the Old English 'wella' meaning a spring or well. The second element can mean simply 'place', therefore, Welling is the place of the spring. The spring could have been that rivulet which feeds Danson Lake. An alternative rendering is from the family of Radolphus Willing of Bexley who resided there in 1301.

East Wickham first occurs as 'Estwycham' as early as 1284. The name means a dwelling place or settlement, and it probably began as a farmstead created in the early stages of the Anglo-Saxon era. 'Dansington' was the medieval name for the estate later known as Danson, and had its origin in the Old English 'Denesiging', the farmstead of Denesige. It lay to the south of Welling, extending eastwards to the line of modern Danson Road, and southwards to Blendon and Blackfen.

Upton comes from the Old English 'Uppe Tun', meaning a farmstead built high up. Brampton came from the Old English 'Brom Tum', meaning a farmstead where broom is grown. In 1301 it was known as Bromton and in 1327 Brompton. Wansunt has its origin in 'Want', a person and 'funta', a spring.

**Medieval Times**

The development of Bexley village took place around the court lodge, the administrative centre for the manor on the site of the existing Manor House close to St Mary's Church. From the ninth to the 16th centuries the archbishops of Canterbury were non-resident lords of the manor. Their demesne lands were farmed first through the services of the villagers, and from the late 14th century by leasing the demesne to tenants. The chief manorial ploughlands probably lay where the farmland did until recently, on the south-west and north-east sides of the village, beyond which was woodland and heath providing timber, fuel and rough grazing for the lord and his tenants. The fields themselves were scattered widely so that the appearance from the air would have been that of a patchwork. The three-field system so typical of the Midlands never obtained in Bexley, nor in Kent itself. The villagers were mainly peasant farmers, working the flat ploughlands along the side of the river Cray, and growing wheat, barley, oats and rye. Many who cultivated the demesne lands were hired labourers working under the direction of the reeve (the local overseer). Away to the north and west lay the open scrubland of Bexley Heath, used for common grazing. The highway from London to Dover (now the A207) followed the line of the old Roman road. Pilgrims bound for Canterbury 'the holy blisful martir for to seke' as Chaucer put in his *Canterbury Tales*, would have passed along the old broadway.

Wat Tyler on his way from Dartford to Blackheath at the head of the Peasants' Revolt led his men across the Heath. In 1415 travellers of a different kind would have been seen moving across the Heath. Field workers in Welling watched the passage of the victorious army of Henry V returning from the Battle of Agincourt to London.

Tracks through the woods led to the isolated hamlets of Blendon, Danson and Upton. Brampton, Bridgen and Wansunt joined the earlier hamlets as tiny centres as the population slowly increased.

Every year on Holy Cross day (14 September) a fair was held in Bexley. This annual event continued until the last century and was then held in a field at the west end of the village, probably adjacent to where the church of St John the Evangelist is now to be found. In 1956 some excavations in the garden behind Cray House, next to the mill, uncovered the remains of a tile-built oven and hearth associated with pottery dating from the 13th century. Fragments of pottery louvres were also found, demonstrating that a medieval building had occupied this site. When the former Co-operative Stores (nos.40-2) were being enlarged in the High Street, pieces of medieval pottery were dug up. All this archaeological evidence suggests that the built-up part of medieval Bexley extended at least from the church to the present Station Approach. By the end of this period the Manor House, east of the church, standing on the site of the court lodge, had been reduced to the status of a farmhouse. Bexley Park Wood, to the west of the village, almost certainly derives its name from the fact that it was part of an enclosed deer park used by the lords of the manor. Such parks were normal features of estates held by ecclesiastical landlords and by aspiring gentry. An area within the manor south of the Dover Road and east of Midhurst Hill was known until recently as the Warren. This name would have preserved the memory of a time when rabbits were encouraged to breed there on the gravel slopes to provide fresh meat for the lord and his followers. It is significant that Henry Castelayn, keeper of the arch-bishops' parks in the 15th century, resided in Bexley. In the woods and fields to the south and east of the village were, until recently, so-called 'deneholes', consisting of deep shafts with little galleries radiating from the bottom. Nearly all have now been filled in but in the 19th century there was much speculation as to their origin. One belief was that they had been dug as refuges from the Danes (hence the name 'deneholes'), but in reality they were dug to obtain chalk to spread on the fields in order to increase the soil fertility. Others were dug in the 18th century, many by Durham coalminers who had travelled to the south, but many dated from the late medieval period.

Bladindon Court (later Blendon Hall) was built in the 13th century. Henry and Eadwin of Bladindon were prominent tenants of Bexley manor before King John signed the Magna Carta. The names of two medieval lords of the manor of East Wickham have been commemorated in local street names on the modern council estate. Burnell Avenue recalls Robert Burnell who died in 1292 and was Bishop of Bath and Wells, and also Lord Chancellor from 1274 until his death. He held 81 other manors, so was unlikely to have been seen often in East Wickham. The estate went to Sir William Lovell whose grandson, Francis, inherited. He was a supporter of the imposter to the throne, Lambert Simnel, in a challenge to Henry VII. Lovell Avenue commemorates his association with the district. Dansington is mentioned as early as 1284 in an archbishop's survey. There is no mention of a house but there were seven tenants of the archbishop holding 17 acres between them—very small holdings indeed!

## The Tudor Period

The 16th century marked several changes in the district. The manor of Bexley passed to the King in 1537. Archbishop Cranmer passed the manor to Henry VIII in exchange for another. The demesne land was leased to Sir John Champneis, a London merchant. He built Hall Place in part from building stone from monasteries which had been dissolved by Henry VIII (it was later added to by Sir Robert Austen in 1660). There is a monument to the Champneis family in St Mary's and also a wall brass in memory of Thomas Sparrow, *alias* Lamendby, who was the deputy reeve to the manor. His name is perpetuated in Lamorbey, now part of Sidcup. In this period brick was more widely used and no doubt many of the older houses had new brick chimneys built into them. There is a record of tiles being manufactured in Tile Kiln Lane and in the building accounts of Henry's manor house at Dartford there is an entry of the purchase of 3,000 bricks at five shillings per thousand from John Williamson of Bexley. Probably the red bricks still making up the wall between the churchyard and High Street House came from such a local source. It is likely that the earliest parts of the *King's Head* date from this period as it is basically a timber-framed building with a strutted roof typical of those times. In 1562, the manorial rights of East Wickham were purchased for £400 by Sir John Olyffe, an alderman of London and a Merchant Taylor. Both estates were now in the hands of merchants, reflecting the decline of the influence of the church as landowners. Sir John is remembered by the modern street name of Olyffe Avenue.

King Henry came to Welling in 1511 with his Queen, Katherine of Aragon. They celebrated May Day in the woods at the bottom of Shooters Hill, while staying at Eltham Place. The festivities were planned by the captain of the King's Guard who dressed up as Robin Hood. How the yokels must have watched and wondered at seeing the King, who in those early days of his reign was handsome and not the bloated figure of his later years. On Shooters Hill in 1588 a beacon was made ready to signal the approach of the Spanish Armada. This would have given warning to London and to a wide area of north-west Kent. In 1571 Dansington passed in to the hands of the Parker family and was leased to a Richard Cowper. The farmhouse would have been small and timber-framed and nestling by the stream in the little valley that was later to be turned into the lake by Capability Brown.

## The 17th and 18th Centuries

There is some evidence of involvement in the Civil War on the Royalist side. Parliamentary forces encamped upon the Heath at various times. When the war ended a number of Kentish men drew up a petition against Cromwell's government. Rebel factions captured Rochester. They retreated to Maidstone and, following their defeat on 1 June 1648, they made for London crossing Bexley Heath. They were harried by Thomas Fairfax and skirmishes were fought upon the Heath and two Bexley suspects, Richard Wood, a chandler, and George Cooke, were rounded up by Oliver Cromwell's men, and heavily fined. Sir Edward Brett, an adventurous cavalier officer, lived in Blendon Hall. A summary of his history may be seen on his monument on the north side of St Mary's. Several fine houses were built in the village at the end of the 17th century. No. 57 is a good example of the architecture of that time in dark red brick with a two-storey porch. The date, 1676, can be clearly seen on the north-west corner. Cray House, next to the bridge over the Cray, dates from the same period. Opposite is a row of cottages which also date from the same year.

In the next century Styleman's Almshouses were built in 1755 by John Styleman who lived at Danson. The 12 cottages remain, although modernised, and fulfil their charitable purpose of providing homes for poor families in Bexley. No. 123 in the High Street, next to the churchyard, was built in 1761 by the antiquarian John Thorpe, on the foundations of an earlier house.

The historian, Edward Hasted, writing in about 1775, styled Bexley village as a town. 'There are many handsome modern-built houses, inhabited by genteel families of fortune.' He described the soils as various, the most prominent being gravel with stiff clay. 'A great part is poor and barren excepting the vale by the river, and much covered with heath and furze.' We learn from him that James I granted the manor to William Camden, antiquarian and Clarenceux, King of Arms. He died in 1623 and left the estate to Oxford University. There is a public house named in his memory in Avenue Road, Bexleyheath, and there is Camden Road in Bexley. We hear for the first time of Brampton Hall on the northern boundary of the Heath, in which lived Francis Vanhagen, a London merchant, at the time of Hasted. By 1830 the gardens were very extensive and greatly admired. It must have been an isolated site. We also hear of Bourne Place, a small, yet elegant house near the spot where the Shuttle joins the Cray. The *Black Prince* and *Forte Post House* now stand on the site. But the most important house to be built in the 18th century was Danson Mansion. It is important because it is one of the few surviving Palladian-style buildings. It was built by Sir Robert Taylor between 1763-8 for Sir John Boyd, a director of the East India Company, and the estate was landscaped by Capability Brown. The stables were added later. At the time of writing there is hope that both the Mansion and the stables may be restored to their former beauty by English Heritage.

In the book *Bexleyheath and Welling*, written in 1910 by the Rev. F. De P. Castels, assistant curate of Christchurch, Bexleyheath, there are several references to highway-men. He tells the story of a Dartford miller, John Hands who, in 1788 was driving late one evening down Bexleyheath Hill (presumably the hill down to the Crayford gas-holders). He was attacked by three footpads. One tried to seize the bridle of his horse but Hands shot him. When men from Crayford inn went back to verify the story they found the robber mortally wounded. Then there is the remarkable story of Dr. Latham, a Bexley surgeon, who was attacked one night by a highwayman. The doctor shot and killed the man and with the aid of his servant put the body into his coach, and buried it in his garden before dawn. An 18th-century newspaper reported, 'we are informed that Bexley Common hath for a fortnight been so infested with highwaymen and footpads as to render it unsafe for travellers to pass after sunset'. There was a gibbet at the corner of Gravel Hill and Watling Street to hang executed robbers in chains as a warning to others.

But not only robbers came to the Heath. John Wesley wrote in his diary on 20 October 1753, 'Feeling sick I stopped at Welling and rested an hour'. Again in 1771, when aged 68, 'I preached once at Welling to a larger congregation than I have seen there for many a year and many seemed uncommonly affected, particularly one young gentlewoman, who had never heard of this preaching of this kind before this evening'. The Rev. George Whitfield, another member of the Methodist revival, was friendly with the vicar of St Mary's and preached there on more than one occasion until stopped by the bishop of Rochester for being 'too enthusiastic'. He had more success on the Heath where on 5 June 1749 he spoke to a large crowd (300 in all) by the pond opposite the *Golden Lion*. His listeners were a motley collection of travellers, farm workers, gypsies and villagers.

John and Charles Wesley also had friends in Bexley for they stayed with the Delamottes of Blendon Hall.

It was the presence of so many squatters and disreputables on the Heath that led to its enclosure in 1819. Many were attracted to live on the Heath by the prospect of work in the factories and workshops of Crayford where the manufacture of calico and the tanning and paper industries were thriving. Others came to the Heath for less honest reasons as has been recorded.

**The 19th Century and Bexley Village**
Bagshaw's *Directory of Kent* sheds some interesting light on the size and occupations of the population of the whole area in 1847. There were 779 houses, five churches or chapels, 14 inns or taverns, 13 beerhouses and 13 schools (most of which were private). The list of trades and craftsmen included: 11 bakers, 6 blacksmiths, 4 booksellers and stationers, 15 boot and shoe makers, 2 brewers, 9 bricklayers, 11 butchers, 2 cabinet makers and upholsterers, 7 carpenters and wheelwrights, 2 charcoal burners, 3 chemists and druggists, 2 circulating libraries, 3 coal and wood sellers, 3 corn dealers, 3 cornmillers, 4 dairymen, 20 farmers, 2 fire and life officers (insurance), 11 grocers and drapers, 3 hairdressers, 2 horse and fly proprietors, 2 ironmongers, 5 linen and woollen drapers, 31 market gardeners, 3 milliners and dressmakers, 5 plumbers, glaziers and painters, 13 shopkeepers (unspecified), 2 straw hat makers, 3 surgeons, 3 tailors, 2 clock and watch makers, 4 carriers.

Note the number of market gardeners. Maps of the 19th century show that much of Bexleyheath after enclosure was given over to market gardening, the produce being destined for the London markets.

The railway came to Bexley in 1866 with the opening of the Dartford loop line and the construction of the brick arches to carry the line over the High Street. There were only four objectors of whom only one was a local resident, John Frances Austen of Hall Place. The others were Charles Augustine Smith, secretary to the Trustees of the New Cross Turnpikes, and officers of two rival rail companies, the London, Chatham and Dover and the Sevenoaks Rail Company. There is a letter from the surveyor of the South Eastern Railway (the builders), a Mr. Edward Ryde, reproduced in the minutes of the St Mary's Vestry of 22 September 1864. It asks if the parish authorities will sell a field as this would save the company the cost of building a bridge. The minutes show that the decision was passed to the vicar and churchwardens. That these gentlemen did not agree to sell the field is proved by the existence of the bridge over the High Street! Had the glebe field been sold, together with other non-church land, the course of the railway would have gone behind the church and probably crossed the road near Vicarage Road by a level crossing. One result of the railway was to turn Bexley into a residential district for people working in London, a phenomenon also occurring in neighbouring Sidcup. A number of substantial middle-class houses sprang up on the north-west side of the village in the area of Parkhurst Road and Salisbury Road, and also to the east on the high ground at Coldblow (Wansunt). There is a rare Victorian pillar box in Parkhill Road known as the Penfold Hexagonal which was placed there in the 1870s. A new church, St John's, was built as a chapel-of-ease to St Mary's in 1881 to cater for the spiritual needs of the new residents. Other terraced houses were built for the less affluent, leading off from the High Street. A brewery was opened in Bourne Road (Reffell's). A Congregational church was built at the junction of the High Street and Hurst Road in 1890 and the Freemantle Hall was opened in 1894. The Victoria Homes in Bourne were built in 1897 to mark the year of Queen Victoria's Diamond Jubilee.

**The 19th century and the Heath**
At the beginning of the 19th century houses on the Heath or its borders could have been counted on the fingers of one hand. There was Brampton Place to the north, Blendon Hall to the south and the *Golden Lion*, a coaching inn, in the centre on the old Dover Road. The present public house of this name was rebuilt in 1901, but the original building dates back to 1710. There was a wooden dwelling beside the great windmill which dominated the landscape where the present bus station in Erith Road stands (it is possible that the Grade 2 listed building, no. 62 Woolwich Road, may be this wooden building, having been moved there on wheels). It is believed that John Dann, the miller from 1830, had wheels put on the house to prevent it being attached to the freehold. The *Old Crook Log* was a common beer shop, just inside the turnpike gate. Warren Farmhouse was built on a small hill, the site of which can be seen and climbed from Midhurst Hill, off Latham Road. The people of Bexley had no real control over the Heath. The soil belonged to the manor but surrounding freeholders were allowed pasture, wood cutting, turf and cultivation. As we have seen, there were many squatters and travellers on the Heath and the local property owners, worried at the uncontrolled development that was taking place by newcomers who paid neither rent nor rates, decided to plan a course of action. On 17 June 1814 a Bill to enclose lands in the parish of Bexley was tabled. When the Enclosure Commissioner published his awards in 1819, it was found that some of the recipients had already sold land allotted to them. Many of the purchasers were hoping to make money by building houses to sell or to rent out. One of these, Nathaniel Josling, licensee of the *Golden Lion*, went bankrupt in 1820 after over reaching himself in land speculation. The enclosers met in the *King's Head* and 115 received grants of land in lieu of rights in common. Two ponds, one opposite the *Golden Lion* and the other at the end of Church Road, were to remain public for the watering of cattle. The Commissioner, Thomas Brown, set out six public carriage roads and nine private ones and several public footpaths. The public roads were: the Dover Turnpike (renamed the Broadway), Erith Road, Mayplace and Crayford Road, Long Lane, Lion Road and Bourne Street Road (Gravel Hill).

The public footpaths were: Woolwich Road, Crown Street, Station Road (Pincott Road), Oaklands Road, Bostal Row and Upton Road.

The *Maidstone Gazette* of 28 October 1817, had this to say:

Bexley Heath which was formerly a dangerous wilderness is now become a village. Several handsome houses and shops have been lately erected, which have given an air of cheerfulness to the neighbourhood, and rendered communication between Welling and Crayford, and Dartford and beyond, more easy and agreeable.

The original settlement was around the Market Place. The Market House (only recently demolished after fire) was built in 1831 by John Smith, a wealthy banker living in Blendon Hall. It had 14 cast-iron stands for the sale of fruit and vegetables. In later years it was used successively as a Sunday school, mineral water factory and garage. The district was now known as 'New Town' or 'New Bexley'. The early settlers were poor. Some made brooms from the broom grown on the heath. The early inhabitants were nicknamed Broomdashers! But not everyone liked the new enclosures. William Cobbett in his *Rural Rides* wrote grumpily in 1821:

The land, generally speaking from Deptford to Dartford, is poor, and the surface ugly by nature, to which ugliness there has just been made ... a considerable enclosure of the common, and by the sticking up of some shabby genteel houses, surrounded with deal fences and some things called gardens, in all manner of ridiculous forms, making altogether, the bricks, hurdle rods and earth say—here dwell vanity and poverty.

The Dover Road across the Heath bore more and more traffic. This was to be the golden age of the mail coach. Outside passengers paid three pence a mile; inside paid five pence. A barmaid at the *Golden Lion* reckoned that as many as 48 coaches passed in one day as well as many post chaises etc.

Church-going and schooling were viewed as important by the local dignitaries. The Heath dwellers could only attend St Mary's in the old village and the children the new National School (opened in 1809) in Bourne Road. Many did not attend church or send their children to school. Dissenting chapels sprang up. The Baptists met in a small cottage opposite to where the old Council Offices were to be sited, and in 1833 they built a humble chapel. In 1835 a chapel-of-ease of St Mary's was built at the top of Oaklands Road. It was not until 1866 that Bexleyheath became a separate parish. The land was given by John Smith of Blendon Hall. In order to build it a parish gravel pit had to be filled in. The architect was Mr. Robert Browne of Greenwich who used a silver trowel when the first stone was laid in the presence of the archbishop of Canterbury. The builder was Mr. Strong Junior of Welling, a noted social reformer. The chapel served the Church of England on the Heath until it was pulled down in 1877 when Christchurch was built in the Broadway. The steeple survived to become a well-known landmark for a number of years.

Remains of old headstones may be seen under the trees by the new roundabout. Opposite stands the Trinity Baptist Chapel. This was erected in 1865 in the Grecian style and remains one of Bexleyheath's important buildings. In 1848, a local stationer named John Lovelace put up a small public hall with the grandiose name of the 'Athenaeum'. This has had several changes in use but it is now part of the trading complex in Pincott Road opposite the entrance to Marks and Spencer and the shopping centre. The building of Christchurch was fraught with difficulty. It took many years to raise the money necessary for its completion and the vicar, who carried the burden and who died at the early age of 43, was the Rev. William Pincott. He was so well-thought-of by his parishioners that a drinking fountain and horse trough was put up in his memory in the Market Place. Later the fountain was moved to a situation by the church. Station Road (so called because before the coming of the Bexleyheath line the nearest station was Bexley and the quickest way on foot was down Station Road and over the fields) was renamed Pincott Road in his memory. Christchurch is built in the English Gothic style with an open Memel timber roof. The external walls are of hassock stone faced with Kentish ragstone and random coursed. It is dressed with Bath stone. The stained glass elsewhere in the church was destroyed by enemy action in the Second World War, but much has been replaced.

The most famous house in what was soon to be known as Bexleyheath (after Blackheath which was so respectable) is the Red House. It was built in the orchards of Upton by Phillip Webb for William Morris, that remarkable Victorian designer, architect and early socialist. Completed in 1859 in time for the reception of him and his wife, after their marriage, they only lived there five years.

By 1851 the coaches had ceased to run which affected Bexleyheath a good deal. The nearest railway was at Abbey Wood. The line to Bexley via Sidcup was not open until 1866 and the Bexleyheath line was not even a thought in a developer's head. Local horse-drawn omnibuses began. There was Stoneham's to Dartford and Munyard's to Woolwich. If you needed to get to London you had to engage a fly or take the bus to Woolwich and catch a train from the Arsenal station. The census of 1881 showed that the 'New Town' had far outstripped the population of the village. The total population of the area was 8,793 of which two thirds lived on the old Heath. 1883 saw a new development—the opening of the Cottage Hospital in Upton Road. The site was given by Mr. Bean of Danson. Bean had acquired the Danson estate in 1863, and was to be the entrepreneur of the Bexleyheath railway line. Other notables who lived in Bexleyheath were the novelist, Hall Caine, who lived in Aberleigh Lodge next to the Red House and Sir Charles Tupper KCMG, the Canadian statesman, who lived in the Mount (where the golf course is now).

In the *Crook Log* area a number of large middle-class houses developed, notably along the Broadway and in Avenue Road. The *Crook Log* itself blossomed into a well-known stopping place for carriers and other travellers. Charles Harper in his book *The Dover Road*, published in 1895, writes:

> The *Old Crook Log* inn is the only public house here that has a history of more than 50 years, and this roadside public house is remarkable, not so much, perhaps, on account of its age—which is, indeed, very considerable—as by reason of the curious bid for custom, the landlord makes of holding a free Natural History Exhibition of live birds and animals in his back garden, where monkeys, peacocks, owls, cats, canaries, bats, foxes, and others lead wretched lives, stived up in small cages, and create an effluvium whose strength must be smelt to be believed.

### Bexley, Bexleyheath and Welling in the early 20th century
Bexley continued to grow at a modest rate. Some fine houses were built along Parkhill Road backing onto Bexley Park Woods. More modest villas and terraced houses were built along Bourne Road, reaching out towards Bexleyheath.

A landmark in Bexleyheath was the opening of the Bexley tramway on 1 October 1903. The route ran from Plumstead through Welling and Bexleyheath to Northumberland Heath. Later it was linked to Erith and Dartford, the line forking at the Clock Tower. The first trams were open top four wheelers with room for 22 passengers inside and 30 on top. To protect yourself from rain on the open deck there were canvas aprons fitted to the seats with which to cover the legs. The trams were replaced by trolleybuses in 1935. Another landmark in Bexleyheath was the building of the Clock Tower in the Market Place in 1912 to commemorate the coronation of King George V. The design was chosen in a competition and the winner was Mr. W.M. Epps. It cost £150 to build.

The conversion of the Public Hall (1870) into Pease's Perfect Pictures, later the Picture Palace in 1913, at the junction of Mayplace Road West and Chapel Road marked the advent of the cinema. In the same year the New Cinema soon to be known as the Broadway Cinema was opened opposite Christchurch. It is now the premises of Kwik Save.

After 1900 Bexleyheath became an important dormitory area for Thameside workers. Some 1,500 houses were added between 1880 and 1920 thus doubling the housing stock. Development was linear, along the Broadway and on the Oaklands and Sandford estates south of the Broadway. These were for lower middle class and artisan families. In Welling and East Wickham estates were built for manual workers where small units of land were near to tram routes. The tram provided cheap and reliable transport from Bexleyheath and Welling to Woolwich and Plumstead. The Woolwich Arsenal was the chief employer but there were also cable and electrical works on the riverside. Reports from the Tramway and Lighting Committee of the now Urban District showed that office workers and shoppers were using the services as well as factory workers. The newly-built Bexleyheath line to Dartford (1895) did not attract London-bound commuters initially in the same way that the other railway lines in the south-east did. East Wickham continued to host farmland and there were a number of brickworks. During the First World War the output of arms and ammunition from the Arsenal expanded greatly and there was a corresponding expansion of the workforce. To accommodate this growth of population a huge settlement of huts, built in neat rows, was set up in East Wickham, south of the old church and on the west side of Wickham Lane, south of Wickham Street. These hutments were still in use for many years after the Second World War until replaced by council housing. There were several churches built in Welling. An iron church was provided for the established church by Mr. Alfred Bean of Danson Mansion in 1869, on what is now the south side of Welling Corner; and the Methodists first meeting in a cottage in Belle Grove Road, also erected an iron church in 1901 next to the railway line where it crosses the road.

**Bexley, Bexleyheath and Welling after the First World War**
Bexley village changed little but new estates grew up to the north, east and west. Only the flood plain of the Cray to the south of the village remained unspoilt. New housing cut further into Bexley Park Wood. The Blendon Hall Estate was sold for development in 1929. New Ideal Homesteads acquired some of the land and that of the Vansittart land to the south and built densely to the acre in groups of terraces, but smaller builders put up better homes closer to Bridgen and Blendon Road. Ideal Homesteads were powerful enough to persuade the Southern Railway to let them build a station at Albany Park to enable the new estate residents to commute more easily to London. Upton Road was cut by the new A2 trunk road and good quality detached houses and semis filled the gap between Bexley and Bexleyheath. The Mount became the Bexleyheath Golf Course and a variety of housing developments filled the former orchards in Upton, surrounding the Red House with a sea of suburbia. Good quality housing, with low density, sprang up at Coldblow, and in the Danson Road area. The

Danson Estate came on the market in 1920. The highest offer of £35,000 fell below the reserve price and the estate sale was withdrawn. Against the wishes of the trustees the estate was divided into lots at the second auction. The Clerk to the Council, Thomas Baines, raised enough money privately to acquire 220 acres of the central parkland, and persuaded the council to buy it back from him. Thus Danson Park was saved from being covered with houses and became the much enjoyed open space in the district. Bellegrove, a small country seat, was sold and the new housing of the Bellegrove Park Building Estate developed within its exact boundaries. The Little Danson Estate on the south side of Welling High Street was developed similarly within the pre-building boundaries. In Welling plans also took shape to provide massive housing for mainly manual workers. There was a demand for housing from immigrants from Woolwich, Plumstead and Erith. Without government assistance much-needed building could not get started as labour costs and materials were in short supply after the war. Housing for those on low incomes had to be met by the local authority, whereas skilled artisans, foremen and office workers could afford private buying for modest homes. Thomas Edge and Son built 426 houses on 50 acres between Wickham Street and Upper Wickham Lane. This was between 1920-6. The council borrowed £400,000 to finance the enterprise. The large Stevens Estate was built on land formerly owned by Avigdor Goldsmid. The Westwood Farm originated as late as 1875 when the owners, Oxford University, cleared and reclaimed a large area of woodland; one of the largest farms in the district, it covered 398 acres. It had been cut in two by the railway in 1895 and was again cut by the A2 trunk road (1926). This sectioning of the land aided the sale and development by Ideal Homesteads. The central green of the estate marks the site of Westwood Farm buildings, and the nature of the housing reflects the three sections of the land. As with Albany Park, Ideal Homesteads was able to build Falconwood station to enable the new residents of the Westwood Estates to commute more easily to London.

North of the Broadway and beyond the railway line row upon row of cheap private housing was developed. South of Broadway there was also extensive development but of less density. Townley Road and Latham Road were built and only the vestiges of the Quayle-Jones estate land lying between Broomfield Road and Rochcester Way were left by 1939.

Some residents commuted to London, others travelled to Woolwich, and yet others to Erith. By 1939 the Bexley district had become a mature suburb; practically the whole area whether built over or not was primarily devoted to the needs of a suburban population. The influence of the earlier pre-urban landscape had left its mark but the last vestiges of the earlier land-use pattern were quickly disappearing. The Warren farmhouse was already in ruins. To the east, much open land had been saved under green belt legislation (the Halcott Estate and Hall Place Estate).

In Welling the Methodist iron church was replaced by a school hall in 1929 to which was added a brick-built church in 1935.

## The Second World War
The Municipal Borough of Bexley (borough status was granted in 1937) suffered considerable damage during the war. The Vickers factory complex in Crayford attracted numerous bombing raids and often the bombs landed well beyond the target. There was a battery of anti-aircraft guns in Danson Park on the so-called polo field that lit

up the night sky and rained shell fragments all over the district. It was because of their flashes that Danson Park Lake was drained for the duration of the war as it was a good indicator as to position to the German navigators. During the massive daylight raids of August and September 1940 the air fields were the principal targets so the residents had a grandstand view of the aerial fighting. A yellow-nosed Messerschmidt 109 fell into the front garden of a cottage in Wickham Street in October 1940. During the winter and autumn of that year, the Luftwaffe virtually bombed indiscriminately round the clock. The bus station in Erith Road was set on fire and many buses burned out. On 15 October a stick of bombs fell along the Broadway in broad daylight. One fell on Woolworths, another on the 1940 Cleaners shop opposite Christchurch. There were many casualties. The church was turned into a temporary mortuary. King Harold's Way and Abbotts Walk suffered in April 1941 when a parachute mine fell between the two roads. Seventy-seven bungalows were destroyed or suffered major damage and 1,072 properties were damaged by this one missile. Later in the war when the flying bombs (V1's) and rockets (V2's) were launched from the continent further casualties and damage were caused. Altogether there were 155 civilians killed, 678 injured and detained in hospital and 1,372 injured less seriously. There is a tablet in memory of many of these in the cemetery behind Christchurch. Hall Place was taken over by American army units in the later years of the war.

**Since the Second World War**
There has been a renewal of house building. The Halcot Estate has been further developed. There has been a good deal of small scale development in Blendon and along Hurst Road. Large houses in Parkhill Road and adjacently have been demolished to make way for smaller properties. A large new development has occupied land between Hurst Road and Parkhill Road (on land cleared from Bexley Park Wood) in the Camden Road complex. There has been further building in Welling and East Wickham. There has been in-filling and attempts to build on backland where gardens are large or previous developers left space. The creation of conservation areas in Old Bexley, the Red House Lane and the Parkhurst area of Bexley has limited inappropriate development and alteration. The much stricter application of planning permission since Bexley has become a London borough has rightly limited development and usually prevented the removal of what green areas remain. The Borough Development Plan makes Bexleyheath the municipal centre. New civic offices have been built at the eastern end of the Broadway, not far from the site of the old civic buildings and the tram shed. A large indoor shopping centre with a roof car park has replaced the old shops on the south of the Market Place and further redevelopment has taken place to change the road system, pedestrianise the Market Place and a section of the Broadway, and relocate the police station from the corner of Albion Road to the other side of Arnsberg Way. The Regal cinema, next to Christchurch, has been demolished and an ASDA store of controversial design has replaced it.

**Schools**
The National School in Bourne Road (now industrial premises) was opened in 1809 and the tiny National School at Bridgen was opened in 1844. Various premises were pressed into service as church schools and then abandoned when better buildings were acquired. Under the leadership of the Rev. G. Graham, Vicar of Christchurch, a new

National School was opened in Albert Road, Bexleyheath, in 1883 to house 250 boys and 250 infants. This was enlarged in 1887 to house 250 girls. Mr. Graham died at the end of the year and as a tribute to his memory the road in which the schools stood was thereafter known as Graham Road. Mr. William Foster of Shirley, Croydon, provided in his will of 1727 a school for 27 poor children of East Wickham. By 1860 the size had expanded to 78 owing to the settlement of workers from the Woolwich Arsenal. These were all church schools and the local clergy fiercely resisted the building of secular or board schools. But the pressure of population was so great that an election of a School Board took place in 1894 and Upland School was established in Church Road, Bexleyheath. This was soon followed by Hook Lane School, Welling. Senior central schools were introduced after the First World War. In Welling, the Central School in Elsa Road was opened by Lord Sackville in 1923, and the Bexleyheath Central School was opened in 1931 in Graham Road. Westwood Central School soon followed. The Bexley Technical School for Girls was built at the southern end of Townley Road (now renamed the Townley Grammar School). Several primary schools were opened (e.g. Brampton) to serve the children moving into the new housing developments. After the Second World War, many new primary schools were built and Bexley Grammar School was established on land in Danson Park. There were several private schools of which the most notable were Cottingham's and Upton College, both opposite the entrance to Danson Park where the new sports centre now stands. They did not survive the last war, although University School, which replaced Cottingham's, moved to Upton Road South and continued until a few years ago.

**Churches**
Mention has already been made of St Mary's, Christchurch, St Michael's and St John's as parish churches and Trinity Chapel as baptist. As the population exploded in this century new churches were provided. A new St Michael's was built at East Wickham in 1932 to replace the old one which was considered too small. It contains many effects from the old church and has a striking recent addition, an icon depicting Christ the Divine Word of God in Glory, painted in 1973 by a monk of the Greek church, a Russian-born septuagenarian, called Hieromonk Sophrony. In 1969 the old and now redundant church was taken over by the Greek Orthodox and re-dedicated to All Saints. In 1925 the foundation was laid of St John's Church in Danson Lane. St Mary's, on the west side of that curious piece of open land in Welling, Shoulder of Mutton Green, was commenced in 1954. It is a brick-built structure with a thin Lombardic tower. A chapel beside the sanctuary is dedicated to St Thomas Becket on account of his association with the Canterbury pilgrims who would have passed along the nearby main road in times past.

A new United Reform church at Geddes Place was built in the new Market Place complex to replace the old Congregational church that stood on the corner of Chapel Road. St John Fisher Catholic Church was built in Thanet Way, Bexley, in 1974 to a striking design.

**Old Among the New**
Bexley village has many old buildings and remains much as it was 200 years ago. It is within a conservation area and building and alterations are closely monitored by the Bexley Civic Society, a voluntary amenity and pressure group. The society monitors

all development in the district but because of the concentration of the old and the good in Bexley, there is particular concern with what goes on there and in Parkhill Road (also a conservation area). Compared with nearby Sidcup there were few large estates that survived to leave their footprints to posterity. Blendon Hall was demolished, as was Brampton Hall. Only Danson Park and Hall Place have remained as large open spaces. Some open land has survived in East Wickham where the Borough boundary meets that of Greenwich. There is Russell Park between Woolwich Road and Long Lane and Bursted Wood, which is but a fragment of earlier woodland. Churchfield Wood abutting Coldblow is protected by the green belt legislation but is small in area. Bexley Park Wood survives but a shadow of its former self.

The joy of Bexley to those who like walking or horse riding is Joyden's Wood, although much of it lies in Dartford. Once having climbed into the heart of the wood it is difficult to believe that the centre of London is only 13 miles away! The south of the district, that is to say, south of the Broadway, has the better housing, the larger gardens, the greater number of trees and a more undulating landscape. In the past those living in this more affluent area have fought to prevent cheaper housing, more dense to the acre, being developed. Often they have succeeded. The area north of Bexleyheath railway was the last to be developed on open farmland or market gardening land, and has the cheaper housing and greater density to the acre. There is significantly less open space and fewer amenities. This is also true of the linear development on the former Westwood farmland. East Wickham remains curiously different. Though almost swamped by Welling, it still has one foot in the country and reflects that separateness that stems from once being part of the Manor of Plumstead.

Were William Cobbett to return and ride across the Heath, he would be astonished at its growth and prosperity. He would recognise no landmarks unless he were particularly vigilant to pick out the *Golden Lion* under its turn of the century coating. He might perceive the *Coach House* (formerly the *Lord Hill*) and some of the old cottages near Pinnacle Hill. He would rub his eyes with astonishment to see the Woolwich Building Society building, like some eastern pagoda placed at the corner of Erith Road, and at the sight of the *Swallow Hotel* across the road, both a denial of the poverty that he predicted for the enclosure of the Heath. For Bexleyheath and Welling are triumphs of outer suburbia, with little or no industry or office development, leaving Bexley village with all its ancient charm to house, paradoxically, a nucleus of light industry, as well as a plethora of pubs and restaurants.

# OLD BEXLEY

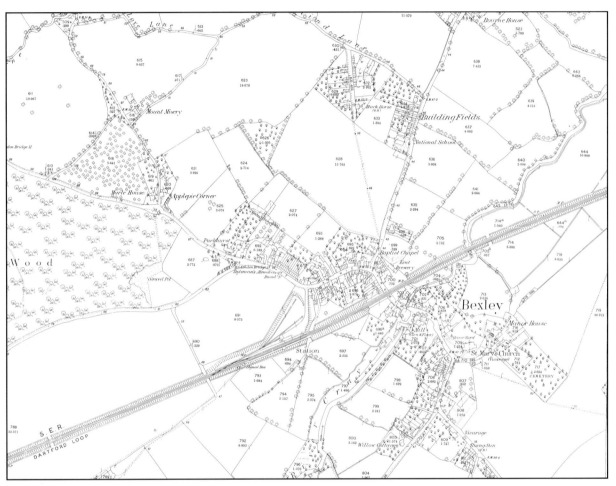

**1** Map of Bexley village. Surveyed in 1862 and 1867. Railway inserted in 1870. Published by Ordnance Survey in 1883.

# Churches

**2** St Mary's Church in 1870. There was a church on the site at the time of the Domesday Survey (1086). It was rebuilt in the 12th century with additions in the 13th and 14th centuries. In 1882 it was restored by Basil Champneys. It has a unique two-stage spire which probably dates from the early 13th century. This is like a cone on top of a pyramid. The interior is full of monuments. Among the most interesting are: a brass of Thomas Sparrow (1513) on the floor to the left of the altar, a large monument to John Styleman (c.1750) on the south wall of the nave, and, on the innermost arch of the arcade, an elegant tablet to Lady Isabel Dashwood of Hall Place.

**3** St Mary's Church in 1972. Note that the room over the porch has been removed. Since then the lych gate has been restored and moved to the south entrance of the churchyard. The oldest tomb is that of the Payne family (1603), which is under the yew tree near the old position of the lych gate. There is a second churchyard to the north of the church, reached by a path running close to the Manor House. This is kept as a conservation area for wild life.

**4** The tithe barn in 1870. It was opposite the church where the church hall now stands. In medieval times the canons of the Augustinian Priory of Holy Trinity, Aldgate, received most of the parish income for its own use, but had to put in a vicar to act as parish priest. After 1215 the canons were to have the greater tithes (a tenth part of the corn and hay produced in the parish), and were to have it collected in a barn of their own, the tithe barn. The vicar was to have the lands and buildings belonging to the parish church, together with other revenues. These would include the lesser tithes (hens and eggs) and offerings at the altar.

**5** The old Strict Baptist Chapel, built in 1845, is now nos. 1-3 Bourne Road. No. 1 is called the Village Baker. No. 3 was Eurosports but is now empty. The ventilator on top of the roof ridge is a reminder that once it was a chapel.

# Houses and Roads

**6** The west exterior of Manor House in 1939. This important old house cannot easily be seen from the road, but there are partial views over the churchyard wall. The southern part is the oldest (probably 18th-century) though there may be elements going back to the 16th century. It is owned by the Chapman family but is at present unoccupied.

**7** High Street House, no.123 High Street, photographed in 1970 whilst unoccupied. The house was built in 1761 on the site of an earlier (probably 16th-century) house. It was the home of John Thorpe, historian and antiquary, from 1750 until 1789. The wall separating the house from the churchyard is part Tudor. On the church side of the wall is a tablet to John Thorpe's wife, Catharine.

**8** High Street House in the snow of 1986 and no longer derelict. Mr. and Mrs. Russell Gray are the contemporary residents.

**9** Bexley village looking east. The old mill is hidden to the right. Note the horse and cart in the river Cray.

**10** The High Street, *c.*1924. The Freemantle Hall has just had a clock added in 1920. The *Kings Head*, just past the Freemantle Hall, is a timber-framed pub, basically dating from the late 16th century. The front part is a late 19th-century extension.

**11** Iron milestone (13 miles to London Bridge), outside the United Reform Church, Hurst Road.

**12** The former site of Reffell's brewery in 1971. The brewery operated from 1874 until 1956. It is now Old Bexley Business Park.

**13** Bourne Cottage. This stood until quite recently near the *Black Prince* and was demolished when the motorway was extended.

**14** Sale notice of Hall Place dated 1912. Note the extent of the estate and the house and farms belonging to it.

**15** The western aspect of Hall Place in 1880. The grounds were not so well laid out as now! It was at this time in the hands of the Dashwood family although they rarely lived there. In the 19th century it was a boys' boarding school (*see* illustrations 31 and 32). The last tenant was May, Countess of Limerick, from 1917 until her death in 1943. During the latter part of the Second World War it was occupied by the American Air Force.

**16** The north front of Hall Place dates from the 16th century when it was built for Sir John Champneis. The southern extension in red brick was added in 1660 by Sir Robert Austen.

HALL PLACE, Nr. BEXLEY.                                                    F. K. 157.

17  Bourne Road at the turn of the century. The photographer is facing towards Crayford. The modern car park for Hall Place is on the right.

18  Bourne Road in 1970 from the same camera position. The Halcot estate on the left has been turned into municipal parkland and housing.

**19** Blendon Hall in 1800. The estate of Blendon (from Bladindon after John and Mary Bladigone) dates back to the 13th century. This illustration shows the Hall as built for Lady Mary Scott in 1763. Humphry Repton landscaped the grounds. Some of his magnificent trees survive between the Sanctuary and Cedar Close.

**20** Oswald Smith of Blendon Hall during the First World War. The present Queen is the great-granddaughter of Frances Smith and Claude Bowes-Lyon. Frances Dora Smith was the daughter of an earlier Oswald Smith. The marriage took place in St Mary's Church in 1853. The Smiths owned a good deal of land in the parish and provided the land for the chapel-of-ease and the market place in Bexley Heath.

21   Blendon Hall gardeners in 1900. Henry James Johnson is the one on the left.

22   The staff of Blendon Hall, *c*.1900.

**23** Blendon Hall being demolished in 1934. It stood approximately where Beechway now runs and the estate of 88 acres ran from Blendon Road to the river Shuttle. The Drive (with the West Lodge still standing) was the main entrance.

**24** Map of Blendon Hall estate following the housing development by D.C. Bowyer and others in the 1930s. The Drive follows the entrance road to the Hall. Some of the gardens to the north end of the Drive contain magnificent trees planted at the time of Humphry Repton's landscaping in 1813 for the banker, John Smith. The lake flowed approximately along the site of Avenue and Beechway.

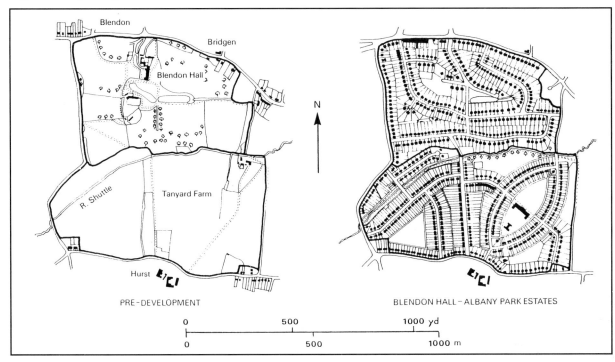

**25** Blendon Cottage in 1951. This was on the north side of Blendon Road where Arcadian Avenue and Arcadian Close are now found.

**26** Bridgen, *c.*1914. The *Blue Anchor* is on the left opposite cottages which are still in place. The *Blue Anchor* was rebuilt on the opposite side of the road nearer to Bexley in 1928. The former pub was used as a café for many years before being demolished to make way for new housing.

**27** The lodge and coach house to Hurst Place and Hurst Place itself on the border of Bexley and Sidcup. Hurst Place remains as a community centre.

**28** Some youngsters pose for a pre-1914 photograph in St Mary's Recreation Ground. Today it is accessible by a single gate off Lesley Close and has minimal facilities and is under-used.

**29** The walk from Bexleyheath to Bexley down Pincott Road, skirting Warren Farm and leading into Love Lane (before the A2 was built), *c.*1923. A footbridge spans the motorway today.

**30** Footbridge over the Shuttle (or Bourne) before the M2 was built, cutting Upton Road in half.

**31**  Tanyard Farm, *c.*1914. The site is under Murchison Avenue. Elmwood Road was the farm entrance from Bridgen. It was part of the Vansittart estate sold in 1933 to New Ideal Homesteads. Whereas the houses built on the Blendon Hall Estate were six or eight to the acre, the New Ideal Homesteads built 12 or 16 to the acre.

# Schools

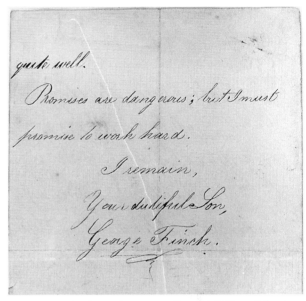

Hall-place, Bexley.

August 10th, 1852.

My dear Papa:

I received my parcel safely on Monday at tea time. I thank Mamma for the cake she sent me, and you for the cricket bat and ball. I hope that you are quite well. Give my love to my Brothers my Cousin, and Mamma, I hope they are all

A 153

quite well.

Promises are dangerous; but I must promise to work hard.

I remain,

Your dutiful Son,

George Finch.

**32**   Copy of a letter from a pupil at Hall Place School to his father, 10 August 1852.

**33**   Bexley National School in Bourne Road, 1910. The school was opened in 1834 and turned to industrial use in 1974. The building to the left was the school hall which was added in the early 1900s.

**34**  A class of 1927 from Bridgen Church of England School. This was also a National School opened in 1844 and closed in the 1970s. It is now a private house. In the 19th century the Church of England fought hard to keep all the local schools under church control and only lost to secular schools as Bexleyheath grew so rapidly.

**35**  University School in Upton Road in 1951. Before the Second World War it was in Brampton Road. The buildings are now the Adult Education Centre. The school was first opened at the Crook Log as Cottingham's Grammar School. When Mr. Cowan bought the school from Mr. Cottingham in 1936 the modest blue blazers were changed to a vivid black and red stripe.

# Railways

**36**  Bexley station in South Eastern Railway Company days, *c.*1890.

**37**  The staff of the station in 1904. In those days the railways were labour intensive. Today with demands to reduce labour costs, video cameras, to give train drivers a clear view of the platform, have replaced the porters, and station masters have disappeared.

**38**   A strawberry train standing at Bexley station, *c.*1905. The area around Bexley was noted for its strawberry fields and special trains were provided in the season for the speedy transport of the fruit to the London markets and beyond. Strawberries are still grown locally but it is now 'pick them yourself'.

# Industry

**39** Workmen at Cousin's forge, Blendon (1896-1915).

**40** Bexley Mill in 1915. Originally built as a corn mill in 1779, it burnt down in 1966. It is now a restaurant, the Old Mill, reconstructed quite closely to conform with the original, with running water of the Cray coursing below the ground floor.

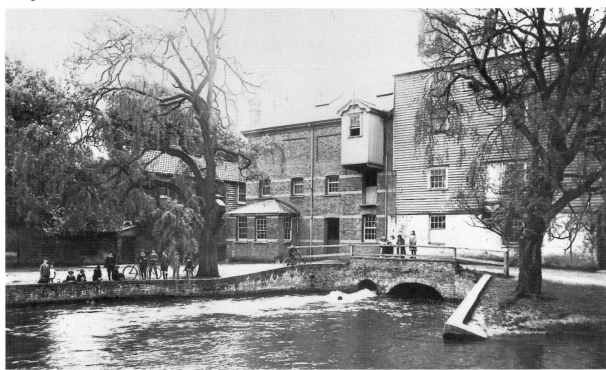

**41**  A Thornycroft steam wagon working for the mill, *c*.1902.

**42**  The impressive workforce of Reffell's Brewery, *c*.1905. In the back row are the boy bottle washers. In the front row are the brewers. On the extreme right of the front row is Stacey, the Fire Brigade Captain. On the extreme left of the front row is the stoker holding his shovel.

# People

**43** William Camden (1551-1623) was an antiquarian, historian and Clarenceux King-at-arms. He became of lord of Bexley manor and left all his manorial interests to the University of Oxford, which accounts for the amount of property owned today by the university in and around Bexley.

**44** Mr. William Freemantle, born in Hampshire and a long-living resident of Bexley. In 1887 he bought Claygate Cottages in the High Street for £600 for the purpose of building a Conservative Working Men's Club and Meeting Hall, and 'for purposes of any kind not inconsistent with Conservative principles'. Five trustees were appointed and Mr. Freemantle laid the foundation stone on 3 August 1894. He began saving crown coins towards a clock which, with added donations, was erected in 1920. Today it is widely used as a village hall.

**45** Dr. Joseph Eagland Walker of Glenthorn, Parkhurst Road, *c.*1912. He was a surgeon as well as a physician and moved to Newlands in Park Hill Road later. He was still living at this second address in 1938 according to the *Kent Directory* of that year.

**46** Newman's Butterfly Farm in Salisbury Road in 1926. Mr. L.W. Newman in the centre. This was a remarkable late-Victorian enterprise where moths and butterflies were bred to be bought by collectors, zoos and laboratories. The founder died in 1949.

**47** L. Hugh Newman, the son, who took over the business until the late 1960s. He was a well-known broadcaster and writer on natural history.

**48** The opening of Hall Place gardens by the Duchess of Kent on 3 June 1952. Alderman H.F. Tanner is looking on (strangely like the late Kenneth Williams!).

**49** Brownie winners of the Bexley Civic Society Children's Art Exhibition of 1983 held in Hall Place. From *left to right*: Rachel Grant, Rebecca Wright, Elisabeth Edwards, Maxine Hort.

# Miscellaneous

**50** Eighty Oak Wood planted at the foot of Gravel Hill in 1980 to commemorate the 80th birthday of the Queen Mother.

**51** Plaque commemorating the planting of the trees.

EIGHTY OAK WOOD

TO COMMEMORATE THE 80TH BIRTHDAY OF HER MAJESTY QUEEN ELIZABETH, THE QUEEN MOTHER, THIS WOOD WAS PLANTED ON 18TH NOVEMBER 1980 BY THE WORSHIPFUL THE MAYOR OF BEXLEY — COUNCILLOR J. HOLDEN.

THESE TREES WERE DONATED BY ORGANISATIONS, FIRMS, AND MEMBERS OF THE PUBLIC THROUGHOUT THE LONDON BOROUGH OF BEXLEY. THE PROJECT WAS ORGANISED BY THE BEXLEY CIVIC SOCIETY IN CO—OPERATION WITH THE DEPARTMENT OF PARKS AND RECREATION.

**52** The bath house dates from *c*.1766, and was originally in the grounds of Mount Mascal. It was a cold plunge house bestride a channel of the river Cray. It was restored in 1990 and is now a Grade 2* listed building. It lies behind a 1930s house in North Cray Road.

**53** The nose cone of a German bomber which crashed on 3 November 1940 in the garden of 16 Wansunt Road. It was a Dornier DO 17z believed to be of 8/KG3 unit of the Luftwaffe. Note the ace of spades on the engine cowling.

# BEXLEYHEATH

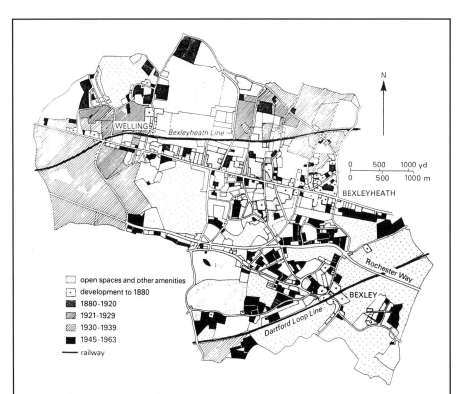

**54** Map showing the development of Bexley.

Legend:
- open spaces and other amenities
- development to 1880
- 1880-1920
- 1921-1929
- 1930-1939
- 1945-1963
- railway

Map labels: WELLING, Bexleyheath Line, BEXLEYHEATH, Rochester Way, BEXLEY, Dartford Loop Line

Scale: 0 500 1000 yd / 0 500 1000 m

**55** Map showing the interrelationship of residential estates with earlier holdings as at 1910.

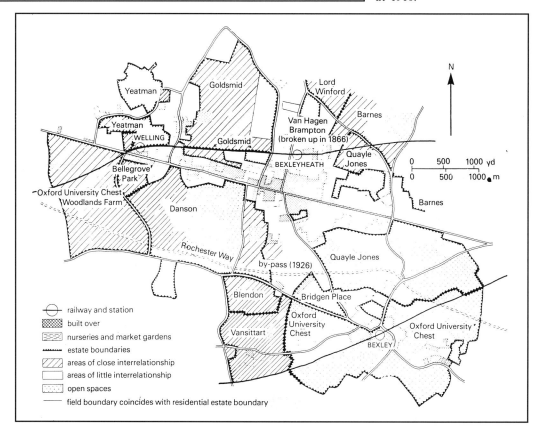

Map labels: Yeatman, Goldsmid, Lord Winford, Barnes, Yeatman, WELLING, Goldsmid, Van Hagen Brampton (broken up in 1866), Quayle Jones, Bellegrove Park, BEXLEYHEATH, Oxford University Chest, Woodlands Farm, Danson, Barnes, Rochester Way, by-pass (1926), Quayle Jones, Blendon, Bridgen Place, Vansittart, Oxford University Chest, BEXLEY, Oxford University Chest

Legend:
- railway and station
- built over
- nurseries and market gardens
- estate boundaries
- areas of close interrelationship
- areas of little interrelationship
- open spaces
- field boundary coincides with residential estate boundary

Scale: 0 500 1000 yd / 0 500 1000 m

# Churches

**56** Old Baptist chapel, Broadway, Bexleyheath. Founded in 1823, it was the first permanent church building on the Heath. It was pulled down in 1956 to make way for a large Co-operative store. This in turn was taken down to make way for a new Trading World building.

**57** The former Wesleyan Chapel in Chapel Road.

**58** Trinity Baptist Church officers. This church was erected in 1868 and still stands opposite the site of the former chapel-of-ease. It is a most attractive building with an Italianate doorcase and four tall Corinthian pilasters surmounted by a large pediment enclosing a circular window.

**59** Chapel-of-ease built in 1835 as an outpost of St Mary's, Bexley. The site was given by the Smiths of Blendon Hall. Part of the site lay within the parish gravel pit which had to be filled in. It was demolished in 1877 but the spire did not come down until 1928.

**60** Christ Church, *c.*1900. Note the undertaker's cart to the left. The church was begun when the Rev. W.H. Pincott was appointed as first vicar to the new parish. It was a good number of years, however, before completion.

**61** Christ Church vicarage erected by Mr. Pincott. It is now no longer used as a vicarage, but has been converted into offices.

**62** The wedding of the author's parents, Leonard J. Mercer and Daisie E. Weaving at Christ Church in 1912. Large hats are obviously the fashion!

**63** John Ridley, Chairman of the Bexley Civic Society, at the 100th anniversary of the death of Mr. Pincott. Mr. Pincott died in 1878 at the early age of 43 brought on by the exertion he gave to the parish and to the raising of money for the church and vicarage. The water fountain in his memory was first raised in the Market Place.

**64** Temporary building of the Roman Catholic Church, St John Vianney, in Heathfield Road, 1951.

**65** Temporary building of St Peter's Church, Pickford Lane in 1951.

# Houses and Residents

**66** George Elms, landlord of the *Royal Oak* in Mount Road, *c.*1940. The pub was given the nickname of the 'Polly Clean Stairs', presumably because his wife was so house-proud.

**67** The corner of Brampton Road and Crook Log, *c.*1890. The tree was taken away when tramlines were laid in 1903. The large house has gone, being replaced by small terraced houses in the 1970s. Today, the intersection is extremely busy and there is a mini-roundabout where once the tree stood.

**68** William and Jane Shove at their doorway of 208 Broadway, *c*.1890. In the 1905 *Jenkins Directory and Advertiser* William Shove Junior is entered as a blacksmith. By 1920 he had become a general smith and the 1929 entry is classified as a farrier and wheelwright. Next in nos. 210-212 was William Hurst, a hairdresser.

**69** The Mount, *c*.1912. A mid-Victorian house which stood where Fairway links Mount Road and Upton Road. The golf club occupies much of the former estate.

**70** H.J. Bristow Esq., resident of The Mount at the turn of the century. He was one-time chairman of the Bexley Local Government Board.

**71** Charlie Ludlow, coachman to Mr. Bristow, posing in a two-horse landau.

**72** Brampton Place in 1900. This 18th-century house was famous in the 1830s-'40s for its extensive and well laid-out gardens. It was on the northern edge of the Heath and quite isolated. The house faced onto Brampton Road and covered the area now occupied by the houses and gardens of Bowford Avenue, Shakespeare Road and Orchard Close.

**73** The old *Crook Log* in 1910. The swimming pool is where the house on the right is located. Earlier there was a toll-gate a few yards to the west.

**74** Market Place, *c*.1905, before the Clock Tower was built to commemorate the coronation of King George V in 1911. The Pincott memorial can be seen before its removal to the side of Christ Church.

**75** A 1920s picture of an early tram by the Market Place. In wet weather passengers on the open top pulled a canvas cover over themselves and clipped it to the seat behind. Penney, Son and Parker's large shop can be seen behind it on the corner of Mayplace Road.

**76** Advertisement for Penney, Son and Parker, one of the best grocers in Bexleyheath. The author remembers being sent there to get sugar weighed out in a blue bag, and butter cut, patted and wrapped in greaseproof paper by the shop assistant who wore immaculately polished leather gaiters.

**77** Mr. George Mence Smith, who opened his first hardware shop at Stanley House in the Broadway. His shop sold tin baths to fit everybody and an attractively priced range of coal scuttles. Later he opened a second shop at 96 Broadway. His entry in the *Jenkins Directory* of 1920 lists him as a wholesale and retail oil and colourman. Subsequently he opened shops in Bexley village, Eltham and other towns in north-west Kent. They all smelt delightfully of paraffin and wax polish. In the 1970s the chain was taken over by Timothy White, which in turn was absorbed by Boots.

**78** Advertisement for D.J. Pitt and Son, carriage proprietors. Taken from *Jenkins Directory* of 1898. Mr. Thomas Jenkins began publishing the *Bexleyheath, Dartford and Erith Observer* on 9 March 1868. His printing office and stationers' shops were on the Broadway where the shopping centre now stands. The *Kentish Times* grew from this venture.

# PALACE Pictures & Varieties

**BEXLEY HEATH.** Lessee and Manager—HARRY QUINTON

Change of Programme every Monday, Thursday and Sunday

## COMING ATTRACTIONS

Every Thursday, Friday and Saturday—Commencing SEPTEMBER 30th

# THE LOST CITY

Col. Selig's marvellous collection of Wild Animals have been made to fit into a film that will thrill and entertain for Fifteen Weeks,

NEXT WEEK—ENORMOUS ATTRACTION—

At great expense we have arranged a return visit of

# MONTAGUE

The wonderful singing fiddler who fiddles with a fiddle.

MATINEES—WEDNESDAY AND SATURDAY AT 2.30

EVERY **EVENING**
Commencing at
**6.30** and **8.30**
Those who do not see the entire Programme (first house) can remain

**SUNDAYS** at 8
Popular Prices

**79** The Palace Cinema showed silent films before becoming a modern cinema in the 1930s. It stood at the corner of Mayplace Road West and Chapel Street. Harry Quinton was a comedy singer who became the cinema owner. In the 1930s he was always to be seen in the foyer welcoming his customers with a flower in his buttonhole. This programme dates from the silent era. It was renamed The Astor and later declined to a bingo hall.

**80**   The Broadway Cinema in 1930. It is now Kwiksave. Next door, at no. 199 Broadway, was the home of the author's maternal grandparents. The lean-to with the advertising panels was the former office of Walter J. Weaving, Registrar for Births, Marriages and Deaths, until his death in 1929.

**81**   Walter J. Weaving, the author's maternal grandfather. He was a prominent Mason and former schoolmaster. He came to the district from Herefordshire in 1881 to be assistant teacher at Bexley Heath National School which was then situated in Pincott Road Hall. He married Emma George, another teacher who came to Bexley Heath at about the same time from Birmingham. Later Mr. Weaving became rate collector, overseer for the poor, as well as registrar.

**82** The author's mother and father before their marriage. The picture was taken in the back garden of 199 Broadway, the home of Mr. and Mrs. Weaving, *c.*1910. The name of the small boy is not known.

**83** The author, aged 10, with his friend, Douglas Jones, in 1933. Douglas's father was a tram conductor. The model of SS *Tiger* was made by the author's father from cardboard boxes given by Mr. Bloom, who kept a dress shop two doors away. Mr. Bloom and his wife had been Jewish immigrants from Poland. Their sons, Arnold and Norman, served with distinction in the armed forces during the Second World War.

**84** Herbert and Son, newsagent and tobacconist, next door to the *Rose*. Sandford's, the greengrocers, to the right. This was a huge shop with all the fruit and vegetables on display from local and London markets.

**85** Queuing for the pictures at the Regal Cinema. It was usual in the new 1930 picture palaces to present live shows as well as films. Robinson Cleaver used to play the cinema organ and became nationally famous. Asda store now occupies the site.

**86** A British Legion parade outside Hide's department store sometime between the wars. The Bexley Heath Shopping Centre is now on the site.

**87** A 1950 photograph of the Red House, built by Phillip Webb in 1859 for William Morris, artist, interior designer and socialist. The site was an orchard and meadow in the small village of Upton. It has been lovingly restored by Mr. and Mrs. E. Hollamby, its current residents. It is now a Grade I listed building.

**88** The Market House in 1972, built by the Smith's of Blendon Hall. It had 14 stands for merchandise. It was later used as a mineral water factory and motor service station. Raised by fire in 1989 it was then demolished.

**89** Demolition of stately Victorian villas at Crook Log to make way for smaller housing in 1972.

# Farms

**90**  Tokens issued instead of money at Hancocks Farm. This farm was north of the railway.

**91**  A local farmers' outing to Clap Board House, Woolwich, *c.*1900. Was the wagonette supplied by D.J. Pitt and Son (*see* no. 83)?

**92**  Haymaking in Pincott Fields between the Broadway and Upton Road.

**93**  The entrance to Baker's Farm, now Townley Road, *c.*1930. It is difficult to realise today, after the growth of Bexleyheath, how close the Broadway was to farmland as late as 1935.

**94** Warren Wood Farm in 1930. A small part of the land is preserved as open space between Broomfield Road and Midhurst Hill.

**95** Pelham Farm, *c*.1930. The tenant farmer was G. McGill. The boys on the horse (Old Bill) are from left to right: F. McGill, Tudor Weaver (his cousin), and A.M. McGill. The farm was sold by Oxford University in 1931. Five and a half acres went to provide land for Pelham School and 11½ acres went to the Ideal Homesteads.

# Schools

**Bexley Heath.**

From Monday, February 2nd, 1829, the Master of the BEXLEY VILLAGE SCHOOL has undertaken a School for Boys and Girls, at the NATIONAL SCHOOL ROOM, on the Heath, on the same Terms of Two-Pence per Week, as the present School; which will be very advantageous to the Heath, as the Bexley Boys already trained, will attend here.

BEXLEY, JANUARY 14th, 1829.

G. A. POCOCK, PRINTER AND BOOKBINDER, LOWFIELD-STREET, DARTFORD.

**96** The opening of the National School room at Bexley Heath in 1829. First in Mill Lane (later known as Mayplace Road West) then in Station Road (later Pincott Road).

BEXLEY AND CRAYFORD Society, FOR THE PROMOTION OF USEFUL KNOWLEDGE.

A LECTURE ON THE WARS OF ENGLAND, WILL BE DELIVERED AT THE ATHENÆUM, BEXLEY HEATH, On FRIDAY Evening, Dec. 1st, 1848, BY A. B. STEVENS, ESQ.

SUBJECT:—The American War, and the Wars of the French Revolution.

The Doors will be opened at Seven o'clock. The Lecture to commence at Half-past Seven.

TICKETS TO BE HAD OF MR. PURDUE, CHEMIST, BEXLEY HEATH.

KIN, PRINTER, DARTFORD]

HENRY DAVIDS, Secretary.

**97** The Athenaeum was built in Station Road (later Pincott Road) for the cultural improvement of the growing population on the Heath. It has survived as part of the Bexleyheath Shopping Hall.

**98** (*above*) Uplands Infants School, *c*.1903. This was the first secular school opened in Bexleyheath by the local school board. An entry from the log book for 2 February 1944 reads, 'A bomb dropped near the school and 100 windows broken', and the entry for 30 June 1944: 'Nights very noisy—pilotless planes roaring overhead. Most children sleep in shelters'.

**99** (*above right*) Top forms of Bexleyheath School, 1930-3. This was a central school drawing pupils from contributing elementary schools. In the second row to the left of the piece of machinery are (*left to right*): A.G.P. Clease B.Sc, C.P. Garner, Deputy Headmaster, Mr. Harris, metalwork teacher. To the right of the machine (*from the left*): E.L. Prescott, Headmaster, H.H.V. Bennett. Standing on the extreme right is the assistant to Mr. Clease.

**100** (*right*) Ellesdon House School, 1931. A private kindergarten run by Miss Kingston (seated centre). Mrs. Gala was her assistant (at the rear). The author is third from right in the back row. Beryl Gage, second from right, centre row. Brenda Maynard, second left, back row. Derek Rueg, third from left, centre row. The school is now no. 302, Broadway, offices of Thomas Boyd White, solicitors.

**101** Upton College Junior School, *c*.1930. Upton College was a private grammar school at the corner of Brampton Road. Its pupils wore red caps and blazers.

**102** Upton College Senior School in 1946, about to be demolished. It was war damaged and never recovered from the trauma of war.

**103** Bexley Technical School for Girls (now Townley Road Grammar School) in 1958. It was built on Pincott Fields in 1934-5.

**104** Inside cover of a book, *George VI King and Emperor,* presented to all schoolchildren in the Borough of Bexley in 1937 to commemorate the coronation of the new king.

URBAN DISTRICT OF BEXLEY

Presented to

*Jean Davis*

BEXLEYHEATH UPLAND CL. JUN. GIRLS SCHOOL

in Commemoration of

THE CORONATION

of

Their Majesties King George VI and Queen Elizabeth

May 12th, 1937

A. G. WILLIAMS,
  *Chairman of the Council, 1936-37.*
  *Chairman of the Coronation Committee.*
W. WOODWARD,
  *Clerk to the Council.*

# Transport

**105** Delivery cart of Premier Mineral Water Co., *c.*1914. The manufactory was in Market House. The mineral water was advertised as 'made in the shadow of the Clock Tower'.

**106**  Plate laying on the Bexleyheath Line near Long Lane Bridge, *c.*1900.

**107**  Bexleyheath Station, *c.*1910. The line from Lewisham to Dartford via Bexleyheath was completed in 1895. Its developers hoped to attract new housing and thereby passenger traffic to London, but for 20 years there was little housing growth, and the main beneficiaries were local farmers. The footbridge used today was not built until 1924. Electrification of the line came in 1925.

**108** The opening of the Bexley Tramways on 3 October 1903. The tram sheds on the left have been pulled down. Second-hand cars now occupy the site.

**109** Bexley Council Tramways in 1910. A children's outing, which may have been a Sunday School trip judging by the cleric near the driver's position.

**110** Bexley Transport (also known as Margo's, after the proprietor) carrying an excursion, c.1923. The garage was in Albion Road. The company was active until the 1980s.

**111** A London Transport tram car, route 46. London Passenger Transport Board took over from the council in the early 1930s and were in turn reorganised into London Transport.

**112** A 698 trolley bus on its way from Abbey Wood via Erith to Woolwich, *c.*1946. The trolley buses were quiet and clean.

**113** The old tram depot in the Broadway next to the former council offices. They were abandoned in the 1930s but used as a centre for civil defence during the Second World War.

**114** The Biddy Brothers Circus on the recreation field (now incorporated into Bexleyheath School) in Edwardian times.

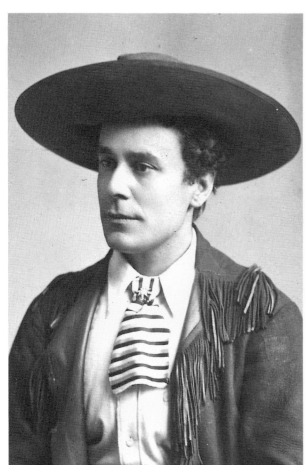

**115** Sequah. A regular circus entertainer prior to 1914 who often came to Bexleyheath.

**116** Mr. and Mrs. Boulter, *c.*1902. He was the sanitary inspector to the Bexley Urban District Council. The Boulters lived in no. 5 Langham Villas, in Standard Road.

**117**  The Boswell family. A.H.T. Boswell, the local photographer, is second from the left in the back row. The family were coachbuilders living at no. 7 Market Place, Bexleyheath.

**118**  Mrs. Baker Beale (with bouquet), chairman of Bexley Urban District Council, presents a baby carriage to the Jubilee Baby in 1935.

**119** Alderman A.J. Franklin JP, the charter mayor of 1937, when Bexley became a municipal borough.

**120** Albert Fisher (Whistling Rufus) was a familiar street musician in the area with his tin whistle in the inter-war years. He died in 1942 aged seventy-eight.

**121** Totty Hardbake, a bag lady of the district before the term was invented. This photograph dates from the turn of the century as she is sitting on an iron seat around a stack pipe in Bexley against the tree that stood at the junction of Brampton Road and Crook Log (*see* no. 67).

**122** Members of the Bexley Civic Society engaged in a litter clear up in 1971.

# War Damage

**123** Air raid on the Broadway, Tuesday, 15 October 1940, showing damage to the Broadway Cinema opposite to Christ Church.

**124** The 1940 Cleaners shop was destroyed and several were killed. A daylight raider dropped a stick of bombs which exploded along the Broadway in the course of the cloudy afternoon of 5 October 1940.

**125** Woolworth's was hit by an oil bomb during the same raid. Many women and children were killed or injured. None of these photographs were released to the newspapers as they were considered by the censor to be too damaging to morale.

**126** Damage to property in King Harold's Way and Abbott's Walk on 16 April 1941. The damage was caused by a land mine dropped in the night by parachute.

# WELLING AND EAST WICKHAM

**127** Map of Welling and Bexleyheath. Extract from the 1892 Ordnance Survey 6 inch to the mile.

# Churches

**128** Church of Christ the Saviour, Upper Wickham Lane. Once St Michael's, it was renamed when in 1967 it became a Greek Orthodox church. It is a small 13th-century building. A new St Michael's was built close by in 1933 and is the parish church of East Wickham.

**129** A modern icon in the church which has attracted a good deal of interest. It was painted in 1977 by a septuagenarian Russian, Hieromonk Sophranus.

**130** The congregation of the Church of England Mission Church by Welling Corner, *c*.1900. The iron church and land was given by Alfred W. Bean of Danson in 1869.

**131** Mr. and Mrs. Robinson with their daughters Jean and Ena. Mr. Robinson was the first pastor of the Welling Methodist Church. The photograph was taken in the family's Tidworth Road garden in 1934.

**132** Opening of the new Methodist Church in November 1935. The stone-laying ceremony had taken place in May of the previous year. The church is a fine, large building which seats 300 people.

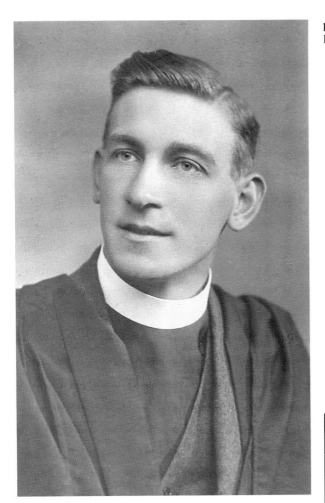

**133** The Rev. Westwood Williams, minister of the churc 1935-6. He died of a heart attack aged thirty-six.

## METHODIST CHURCH
## WELLING
## KENT

### Order of Service

| | |
|---|---|
| OPENING SENTENCES | Sir William R. Codling, C.B., C.V.O., C.B.E., Senior Circuit Steward, Woolwich Methodist Circuit. |
| | HYMN 811. |
| PRAYERS | Rev. E. A. Bastin, William Street, Woolwich, Methodist Church. |
| | REQUIEM. |
| LESSON | Pastor R. H. Fairman, Wesley Hall, Slade. |
| | HYMN 647. |

ADDRESSES :
Rev. Frank Moore, A.K.C.L., Vicar of Welling.
Rev. Walter Taverner, B.A., St. Andrew's Presbyterian Church, Woolwich.

### UNVEILING OF THE MEMORIAL TABLET

ADDRESS :
Rev. W. H. Lawson, Superintendent Minister, Woolwich Methodist Circuit.

HYMN 215.

BENEDICTION .. .. Rev. F. Noel Cooke, H.C.F.

*16th May,* 1936.

**134** The memorial service for Mr. Westwood Williams took place on 16 May 1936. It was a great blow to the burgeoning Methodist church to lose a prominent pastor so soon.

# Houses and Streets

**135** East Wickham House in 1838. It was then the property of Richard Jones Esq. The house was demolished in the 1950s. East Wickham Farmhouse still survives though much hidden by trees and bushes. The façade dates from *c*.1800 but underneath is a 17th-century building. In its heyday of 1900-20 the land was farmed by the Gibsons who had land stretching as far as Brampton Road in Bexleyheath. They profited from the newly-opened Bexleyheath railway which delivered their produce to the London markets.

**136** Tangier House, Welling High Street. This presumably stood to the west of the old *Nag's Head*.

**137** Old cottages in the High Street. Welling is a much older settlement than Bexley or Bexleyheath, having Roman remains.

**138** The old *Nag's Head, c.*1914. The original pub dates from about 1743.

**139** Upper Wickham Lane at the tram passing section. You are looking towards the railway bridge from Welling Corner, *c.*1910.

**140** Bellegrove Road. The *Moon and Sixpence*, formerly the *Station Hotel*, can be seen on the right.

**141** Belgrove Cottage in Bellegrove Road, *c.*1920.

**142** The old *Guy, Earl of Warwick*, *c*.1920. The original name dates from 1730 when Richard Ebbs was licensee. Anne Bean of Danson sold it to Kidds Brewery of Dartford for £5,000 in 1895. The present building dates from 1926. Recently, when McKinley Court was being built on part of the pub gardens, Roman remains were discovered.

**143** Maryville Convent on 4 June 1951. The convent was situated just before Shoulder of Mutton Green, opposite to Welling Way. Since its demise a block of maisonettes has been built on the site.

**144**  Danson Hill, *c*.1786. This fine mansion in the Palladian style was built for Sir John Boyd between 1763-8 by Sir Robert Taylor. The park was landscaped by Capability Brown in 1770 and later the lake was created. It is now a Grade I listed building.

**145**  The mansion showing wings for stables and services. These were removed when the present stables were added *c*.1800.

**146** The stables today, in need of restoration. These have been taken as the logo of the Bexley Civic Society, which was formed in 1971 initially to preserve the stables.

**147** One of the murals in the dining room of Danson Mansion. These were painted by Charles Pavillo in 1766. He later went to Edinburgh to teach art and died young in 1772.

**148**  Chapel House in 1768. This is a conversion, *c.*1700, of an older cottage to form the appearance of a chapel with steeple. It was thus converted to form part of the design for the landscaping of Danson Park.

**149**  The East Lodge leading from the Park to Danson Road. This has been replaced by a modern house and the water fountain has gone.

**150**   The gamekeeper's cottage, *c.*1905. This stood at the entrance from Danson Lane. St John's Church has been built on the opposite side of the entrance.

**151** Mrs. Anna Bean, wife of Alfred Bean. Mr. Bean acquired Danson Park in 1863, having made a fortune as a railway engineer. He was the driving force in building the Bexleyheath Line which opened in 1895. He was also a leading churchman and philanthropist. Bean Road is named after him.

**152** The opening ceremony of Danson Park to the public by Princess Mary, Viscountess Lascelles, April 1925.

**153** Map of Danson Park from the brochure of 1925.

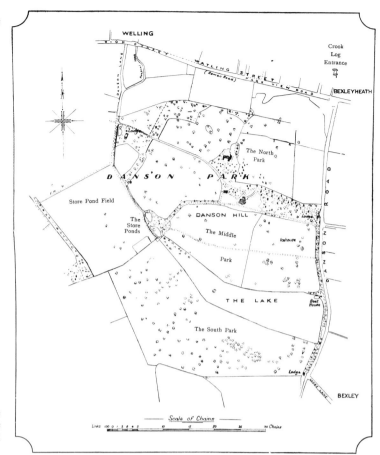

**154** The Grecian Temple which stood where the Boat House Café now stands. The temple has been moved to St Paul's, Waldenbury, in Hertfordshire.

**155** Mr. Hammett and his steam locomotive on the miniature railway on the south side of the lake. A post-1945 photograph. The railway was disbanded in the 1960s but traces of the line remain.

**156** Opening of the Danson Park gates in 1929 by the Lord Mayor of London. The gates were donated by Morris Wheeler JP, Chairman of the Bexley Urban District Council, 1928-9.

**157** Councillor A.J. Franklin turning the first sod on the council's housing estate in Welling in 1920.

**158** The cover of a brochure for the New Ideal Homesteads Ltd., Falconwood Park Estate. This Art Deco cover was designed to attract first time buyers from the 'upper' working class who lived in south-east London and who were socially aspiring.

**159** Drawing room set out for would-be buyers, Type 'A' house at £695.

**160** Front bedroom set out Type 'A' house in 1933.

**161** Westwood Farm from the air, 1934. The farm is cut into three by rail and road. Welling Way can be clearly seen curving its way through Oxleas Wood and on to Eltham. Falconwood Station has yet to be built.

**162** Shoulder of Mutton Green, *c*.1918. Wickham Street is to the right. Shooters Hill water tower to the rear.

# Farms

163  Danson Farm, *c.*1910. Entrance to Bean Road now on left.

164  East Wickham Farm, ploughing in 1900.

**165**  East Wickham Farm, haymaking in 1902.

**166** Rogers the blacksmith at no. 215 Welling High Street. This is now a small one-storey shellfish shop, but the side double doors show its former use.

**167** All that remains of Westwood Farm. A former barn on the Green, Welling.

# Schools

**168** Pupils from Fosters School, Upper Wickham Lane, *c.*1914.

**169**  Hook Lane School when first built in 1908. It was one of the first Board Schools to be built in the district in the face of sustained opposition from the clergy who wanted to maintain their control over education in the local church schools. This school has been demolished to make way for new housing. A new school, also called Hook Lane School, has replaced it.

**170**  Wickham Street School. A class in 1930. Do you recognise anyone?

# Transport

**171** A Bexley tram returning from Woolwich. The driver was unprotected from the weather and had only two controls: a driving handle and a brake.

**172** A no. 89 bus passing the *We Anchor in Hope* in the 1960s. Note the absence of traffic. The day of the motor car *en masse* was to still to come.

**173** A disaster outside the Plaza Cinema, Blackfen, on the Welling/Sidcup border.

**174** A card to Miss Cash of Plumstead, posted in Welling, April 1905.

**175** A card to Miss Larkin of Beckley, Sussex, posted in Bexleyheath in January 1905.

# War Damage

176 Nos. 40, 38 and 36, Cowper Close, Welling, after the fall of a V2 rocket on 10 March 1945. No. 36 had to be pulled down.

177 No. 34 Cowper Close after the V2 had landed.

**178**  Victory Party in Cowper Close, 1945.

# Sources

F.R.H. du Boulay, *Medieval Bexley*, Bexley Libraries and Museums, 1993

M.C. Carr, 'The Development and Character of a Metropolitan Suburb: Bexley, Kent', *The Rise of Suburbia*, F.M.L. Thompson (ed.) Leicester University Press, 1982

F. de P. Castells, *Bexley and Welling,* Jenkins, 1910

L. Dunmow, *Welling Methodists*, 1990

L.A. and L.M. Levy, *Education in Bexley,* Bexley Libraries and Museums, 1971

M. Scott, *Home Fires*, Bexley Libraries and Museums, 1986

M. Scott, *Influence of the railway on Bexley,* M.A. dissertation, Goldsmiths' College, 1994

J.C.M. Shaw, *The Bexley Heath Phenomenon*, Bexley Libraries and Museums, 1983

D. Spurgeon, *Discover Bexley and Sidcup*, Greenwich Guide Books, 1993

P.J. Tester, *The Archaeology of the Bexley Area*, Bexley Libraries and Museums, 1985

P.J. Tester, *Bexley Village*, Bexley Libraries and Museums, 1987

P.J. Tester, *East Wickham and Welling*, Bexley Libraries and Museums, 1991

St Mary's Vestry Minutes, 22 September 1864